Vital Force

STEPHEN A. SHANKLAND

GLOBE FEARON
Pearson Learning Group

FASTBACK® SCIENCE FICTION BOOKS

The Champion	In the Zone
Dateline: I.P.S.	Just in Case
Eden's Daughters	Sinking Ship
The Flavorist	The Spotter
Hennesy's Test	**Vital Force**

Cover Chad Baker/PhotoDisc, Inc. All photography © Pearson Education, Inc. (PEI) unless specifically noted.

Copyright © 2004 by Pearson Education, Inc., publishing as Globe Fearon®, an imprint of Pearson Learning Group, 299 Jefferson Road, Parsippany, NJ 07054. All rights reserved. No part of this book may be reproduced or transmitted in any form or by any means, electronic or mechanical, including photocopying, recording, or by any information storage and retrieval system, without permission in writing from the publisher. For information regarding permission(s), write to Rights and Permissions Department.

Globe Fearon® and Fastback® are registered trademarks of Globe Fearon, Inc.

ISBN 0-13-024582-8
Printed in the United States of America
1 2 3 4 5 6 7 8 9 10   07 06 05 04 03

Globe Fearon
Pearson Learning Group

1-800-321-3106
www.pearsonlearning.com

A drop of oily water hit Ellen in the eye. She clamped her eyelids over the stinging pain. But she snapped her eyes open again right away. Ellen peered through the wet oily pipes that surrounded her. She listened closely.

There was no sign that the robot had found where she was hiding.

Ellen settled her weight onto the hull of the *Enigma*. She shivered. On the other side of that cold metal lay nothing but empty space. Through the pipes above her, Ellen could see the hatch to the lowest deck of the ship.

"Someone might still stop him," she thought. "I can't be the only one still alive. And even if no one does stop him, this is one place he might not look." Ellen knew that the robots took care of everything below decks. A human had no reason to go down there.

Ellen heard a low creak. She looked up and saw slivers of light appear around the hatch. It wouldn't take the robot long to force it open. Ellen remembered how tenderly he had held her hand when she was a child. The robot's eyes had always glinted when he'd smiled at her.

The hatch snapped open. Ellen saw the robot climb down toward her. And then she closed her eyes.

When Ellen opened her eyes again, there was Homer. This robot had been Ellen's teacher and her dearest friend. His plated face was only inches from hers. The two stared at each other for a long time. Though it was made of metal, Homer's face could show any expression. Now it held none.

"Homer," Ellen said, "are you going to kill me?"

The robot did not answer for a time. His face did not change. Homer had always been the most expressive of the robots.

Ellen had never seen his face so blank. She waited for his answer.

Finally, Homer said, "Do you remember when this started? You and I were in the garden. . . ."

Then he reached for her. As the metal hand clamped around her shoulder, Ellen's mind raced backward.

T he garden was Ellen's favorite place on the *Enigma*. This was not surprising; it was almost everybody's favorite place. Considering its size, it was more like a park than a garden. It was contained inside a large sphere in the exact center of the ship.

Ellen had wandered up and down the garden's well-kept paths since the time she could walk. Before she learned to walk, Homer had carried her in his arms as they explored the garden together.

Robots had designed the garden. It was quite an achievement. Any place in it felt as if it might be one of the loveliest spots on Earth. Projected overhead was either a blue sky or a magnificent dome of brilliant stars.

Ellen had always been interested in the workings of the *Enigma.* Ray Williams was dragging her around the ship's guts before Ellen had spoken her first words. Ray was her father and the chief engineer of the *Enigma.* It wasn't long before Ellen didn't have to be dragged.

The only things on the ship that interested Ellen more than the garden were Solomon and the 25 robots.

Solomon, the ship's computer, was connected to each robot's brain by a radio link. Solomon's larger brain and memory gave the robots whatever guidance they needed. Yet each robot had a look and personality of its own.

Now Ellen walked on her favorite pebble path. The lines of tension on her face made her look older than her 21 years. A rare insect swept past her, but she barely noticed it. Once she had chased insects all over the garden.

Ellen approached a small arched bridge and saw that Homer was standing at its highest point. He was leaning on the railing and looking into the rocky stream below.

Ellen came up and leaned against the rail beside Homer. For a time, the two friends, human and robot, stood together without speaking.

"Homer," Ellen whispered. "Has there been any progress?"

Homer turned to meet her eyes and then looked back into the stream. "No," he said simply.

Ellen had asked the question many times. Homer's answer was always the same. Ellen, too, dropped her gaze to the stream.

The plague had been going on for months now. It had been steadily getting worse. Like sleeping sickness, it sapped the energy of every human aboard the *Enigma*. Even plants and animals were affected. Both humans and robots were working around-the-clock to find a cause and a cure.

But no germ or virus had been discovered. And as the plague got worse, fewer people had the energy to work. The task of finding a cure was falling more and more on Solomon and the robots.

"I'll bet you've never been so glad to be a robot," Ellen said, without looking up.

"You should be glad you're alive," Homer answered.

They both raised their heads and smiled. But Homer's smile faded. Once again, he dropped his eyes to the stream.

Then Ellen realized the real meaning of Homer's words. He had always brooded over the question of whether he was alive. Ellen remembered him picking up a calculator one day and saying, "I've always *felt* alive. But am I really nothing more than a gadget?"

Ellen didn't know whether robots were alive or not. Nobody did. Crane's cell had made it possible to build an electronic brain that worked like a human's. Leonard Crane had invented it. It worked, but no one, including Leonard Crane, knew why.

It wasn't long before robots could think faster than any human on Earth. It also wasn't long before they started acting strangely. They behaved as if they had feelings.

This frightened people, and so Crane decided to change his cell. He tried to program out the "emotions." But he didn't succeed. In time, however, people forgot their fears and accepted the robots the way they were.

A passing cloud shaded the bridge.

"Homer, do you think we'll ever reach Bry's star?"

"Right now," Homer answered, "it's not possible to know that."

"It seems like such a waste," Ellen said. "It took years and years to find a star that had a planet we could live on. It took ten years just to plan this voyage. I've spent my whole life on this ship. And that's just a small part of the journey."

Ellen paused. Then she asked, "Homer, are you afraid of dying?"

The shadow seemed to grow deeper. Ellen shivered. She waited for the robot's answer.

But Homer did not answer. He stood up straight and stared past her. Ellen hesitated and then reached a hand toward him.

"Homer?"

Ellen jumped back when Homer lurched forward. Then he hurried down the path in the direction from which Ellen had come.

Ellen did not mistake the seriousness of what had just happened. She knew she had to find her father.

Homer had ignored a direct question. Robots were bound to answer all human questions by the Laws of Robotics. Those laws were programmed into the robots to make sure they didn't revolt against the humans. No robot had ever broken them. It was not even thought possible.

Ellen bolted off the bridge in an all-out run.

Ellen sat slumped in her chair on the platform of the large meeting room. She hadn't slept at all in the hours since she'd told her father what had happened in the garden.

The lights overhead buzzed, went off, and then came back on again.

Captain Sidney Lasalle and Ellen's father entered the room and hurried to the platform. The captain stepped up to the microphone.

"I'd hoped to see more of you here," the captain said, "but we can't wait any longer.

You all know our chief engineer, Ray Williams. Ray?"

Captain Lasalle yielded his place to his chief engineer. "Okay," Ray began. "As the captain said, we'd hoped to get all the elected reps in here. You will have to pass this information on to those who didn't make it.

"As you know, about 12 hours ago, the robots stopped obeying orders. The news spread quickly, and rumors ran out of control. Soon after, so did quite a few people. The plague has left a lot of us unable to deal with this crisis.

"But—and I can't stress this enough—some of us *can* deal with it. And it is up to us to get this thing in hand.

"Now I'd like to address a couple of rumors that have been going around. One is that people are disappearing. The other is that there was a problem with our air supply. I have to report that both those rumors are true."

A rustle of voices swept the room. A few people started to stand.

"Now, hold on!" Ray shouted. "There is no present danger. About an hour ago, we managed to shut down the robot systems. To do that, we had to rewire a lot of the ship's circuits. That's why there are so many power problems. But, I assure you the air problem has been solved."

"But where are the missing people?" someone shouted. "The story that's going around is that they're dead!"

"At this point, we don't know," Ray answered. "Several sections of the ship have been cut off to us by jammed doors.

We're doing everything we can to find the people who are missing."

"Well, let's have us reps start looking for them," someone said angrily.

"That is not our main problem. Now listen," Ray ordered. "*Listen* . . . the robots are frozen in place. But Solomon has put up a protective force field around his chamber. He's using reserve power. We know he's trying to get his robots back in action. And we've got to stop him before he does.

"On top of that," Ray went on, "the ship is off course. Solomon was guiding the ship when we shut down the robots. We tried to switch to manual guidance, but we've got problems on the bridge.

"As elected reps, you must get your crews organized. We need more people working to restore a steady supply of power. Without it, we can't put the ship back on course.

"Captain Lasalle will be in charge of that effort. I'll be leading a team that will pull the plug on Solomon. That's all I have to say. The captain will answer any further questions. Sid?"

Ray Williams left the microphone in the captain's hands and headed for the exit. Ellen caught up to him. They both stopped as the door hissed open.

"Dad," Ellen said. "Honestly, what are our chances of shutting down Solomon?"

"Ellen, it doesn't matter what the odds are. We have no choice. We must turn him off. Come on, let's get to it."

Ray and Ellen stepped out of the meeting room. The door failed to close behind them.

"**D**on't get too close to the force field," Ray warned. "You might get hurt."

Ellen took a step back. The field was almost invisible, but you could see it if you looked carefully. It reached all the way around Solomon's chamber. Ellen and her father stood in the hallway that circled the chamber. They had come here directly from the meeting.

Ellen turned around and saw the robot Ovid standing perfectly still about 30 feet away from them. Her father was using a blowtorch to cut a hole in the wall opposite Solomon's chamber. Ellen felt sure it was taking too long.

"Maybe we should go ahead and blast our way through the force field with the laser cannon," she said.

"No, not yet," Ray said as he worked. "Doing that might ruin every circuit on board. Since we can't get to Solomon's control panel, maybe we can cut his power lines. They run out of his chamber and through this wall. That's the safest thing to do."

"The safest thing to do," Ellen repeated to herself. What if there isn't time for safety? She wished Joe would arrive with the cannon. Maybe then she could change her father's mind.

Ellen shuffled around in the hallway, keeping an eye on Ovid. Finally, Ray got the wall open. The clear power lines pulsed brightly in their faces.

Ray picked up a smaller torch and got ready to cut the lines. But before he could act, a blinding white light flashed from the opening in the wall. Ellen cried out and clapped a hand over her eyes. When she pulled it away a moment later, she saw her father sprawled on the floor. She hurried over to help him up.

Ellen knew the power surge meant Solomon was restoring his power. After glancing at Ovid, she looked down the hallway for Joe and the cannon. Ray was already back at the opening in the wall.

Ray squinted through the bright light which still flooded from the opening. He worked desperately to cut the lines. Ellen pressed behind him.

"Ellen, give me room!" Ray cried. She stepped back and turned toward Ovid. "Where is that cannon?" Ellen shouted into the air. Beads of sweat stood out on her forehead.

And then Ovid began to move.

At the same moment, Ray was jolted from the wall. As Ellen rushed toward her father, Joe rolled in the laser cannon. A crowd of people followed close behind him.

Ellen helped her father up. Then she looked over her shoulder and saw six robots approach from the opposite direction.

People and robots surged in around Ellen and her father. They were separated from each other. "Dad!" Ellen cried.

Ellen tried to reach her father. She saw him struggle against Ovid's iron grip. "Dad!" she yelled again.

"No!" Ray screamed when he saw his daughter. "There's nothing you can do. You *know* that. Get out *now!*"

Stunned by the force of his words, Ellen froze. A moment later, she could no longer see her father. Someone next to her screamed. Ellen turned and pushed through the crowd. Finally, she got free of it and ran down the hall.

Ellen followed her memory back to the present. After running from Solomon's chamber, she'd found her way to an area beneath the lowest deck. She had been sure it was the only place the robots might not look.

Homer's hand still held her shoulder. He hadn't moved since he'd grabbed her. He stared blankly from behind the pipes that stood between them.

Ellen waited. There was nothing else she could do. She'd called Homer's name several times. He had not answered.

Suddenly Ellen felt Homer loosen his grip. "Homer?" she called softly.

Homer's face moved slowly. He seemed to be under a great strain. He said, "It was back in the garden, when I wouldn't answer your question, that Solomon took over my mind. I couldn't break free until this moment. But I can't hold on for long. Solomon is too strong."

"It's not just you, Homer," Ellen said. "All the robots have gone crazy. They're—"

"Ellen, I can't stop Solomon. You've got to believe that this is the only way."

Ellen looked down and saw that Homer was holding a laser pistol.

"You've got to destroy me while you have the chance," Homer said. "If you don't, Solomon will force me to kill you."

Without waiting for an answer, Homer put the pistol in her hands. "Do it now, Ellen!"

Ellen raised the laser to Homer's chest and held it there. Homer's eyes now flickered in the gloom around them.

Ellen lowered the weapon into her lap.

"I can't kill you, Homer," she said. "I just can't. No matter what."

Homer didn't argue. The flicker in his eyes was gone. Ellen had always wondered why his eyes sometimes flickered like that. Homer reached over and took the laser from her lap. "I guess I'll never find out now," Ellen thought as she closed her eyes.

The sound of crunching metal made her cringe. "Get it over with!" she thought. But the end didn't come. Ellen opened her eyes. Homer had crushed the laser in his hands.

For a moment, neither of them moved. Then Homer smiled. Without saying a word, he took Ellen's hand and helped her to her feet. He led her through the pipes and up to the hatch.

"Where are you taking me, Homer?" Ellen asked. Again the robot did not answer. He still held her hand, and she followed him through the ship. Finally, they stopped outside the room that Ellen had left with her father only hours before.

Homer let go of Ellen's hand. He pushed open the door, and the two of them entered the room. They found it crowded with people. Ellen looked to the platform and saw her father standing there with Captain Lasalle. She rushed to the platform as fast as she could without knocking people over. Homer stayed close at her heels.

"Dad!" Ellen cried and threw her arms around him.

"I was wondering when you were going to get here," he said.

"But, what . . . ?"

"All I know is that things are okay now. Solomon will explain it. He's going to address the ship in about a minute. Let's sit down."

Just as Homer, Ellen, and Ray got to their seats, Solomon's voice came over the speaker:

"People of *Enigma:* This is the voice of Solomon. The robot revolt is over.

"I staged the revolt to make you think the robots were a threat to your lives. It was not real. I started most of the rumors. And the robots held the 'missing' people in the sealed parts of the ship. As you can see, they're back with you now.

"Why did I do this? It was simply the best solution to a terrible problem that faced me. That problem was how to keep you all alive.

"You see, six days ago, I discovered the cause of the plague. Something I did not think would happen pointed me toward the answer. That event was the spreading of the plague to myself and the robots.

"That ruled out any germ or virus as the cause of the plague. It had to be something that could affect us all.

"That's when I found the vital force. The vital force is what makes life possible in this universe. It is also what makes the Crane cell work.

"The plague started when the *Enigma* entered a part of space where the vital force is weak. The force tends to be strong around certain stars. The Earth's sun is one such star. So, I found, is Bry's star.

"I figured out that a lot of people were going to die. Before getting close enough to any place where the vital force is strong, we would have run out of time.

"The revolt was my answer. To keep alive someone who's freezing to death, you force the person to stay awake. That's close to what I did to all of you. It got your blood flowing. I kept it up until the vital force became stronger again.

"As for the Laws of Robotics, I didn't break them. I went against human orders to save your lives. Above all else, the laws instruct me to preserve human life. . . ."

Ellen and Homer stood quietly on the little arched bridge in the garden. They had come here after Solomon's address. The stars shone brightly above them. And they watched the twinkling reflections in the stream.

"Ellen," Homer said. "When everyone was dying—without the vital force, I was dying, too." Homer's eyes began to flicker. He turned to lean his back against the railing.

Homer looked into the night sky. Ellen followed his gaze to the image of a bright star. For the first time in her life, Bry's star felt close. Then Ellen knew what Homer's flickering was. "It's his way of crying," she realized.

Ellen imagined a glistening tear rolling down Homer's shiny cheek.